T0016524

SPACE

HANNA KARLZON

Gibbs Smith

Space Coloring Book
Illustrations © 2023 Hanna Karlzon

Original title: *Rymden*

Copyright © Hanna Karlzon och Tukan förlag 2023
Illustrations and design: Hanna Karlzon
www.hannakarlzon.com

First published by Tukan förlag 2023
Örlogsvägen 15
426 71 Västra Frölunda
Sweden
www.tukanforlag.se

English edition copyright © 2023 Gibbs Smith Publisher, USA.

All rights reserved. No part of this book may be reproduced by any
means whatsoever without written permission from the publisher,
except brief portions quoted for purpose of review.

Gibbs Smith
P.O. Box 667
Layton, Utah 84041

1.800.835.4993 orders
www.gibbs-smith.com

ISBN: 978-1-4236-6522-9

Printed in Guangdong, China, in March 2023 by RR Donnelley
Asia Printing Solutions.

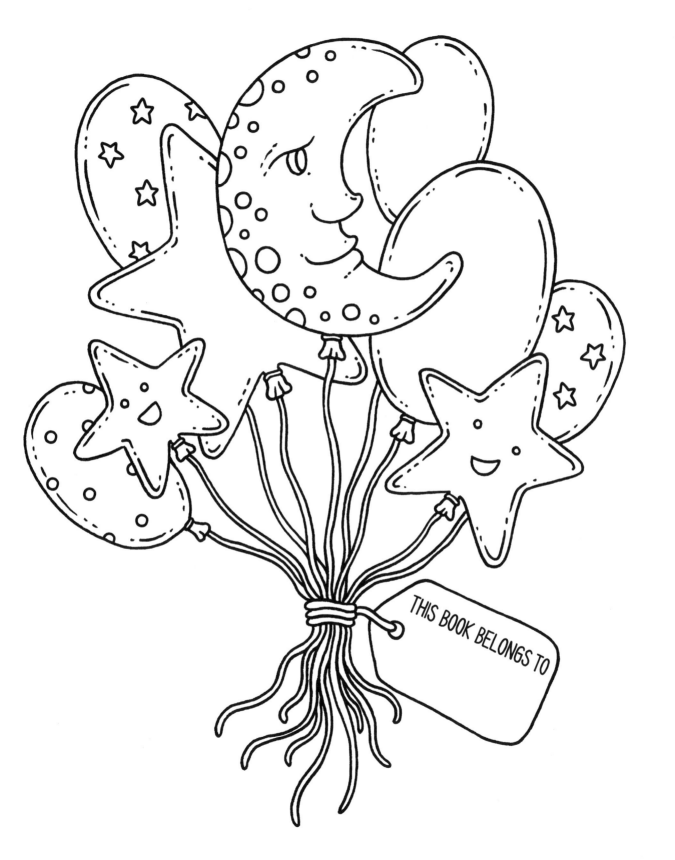

THIS BOOK BELONGS TO

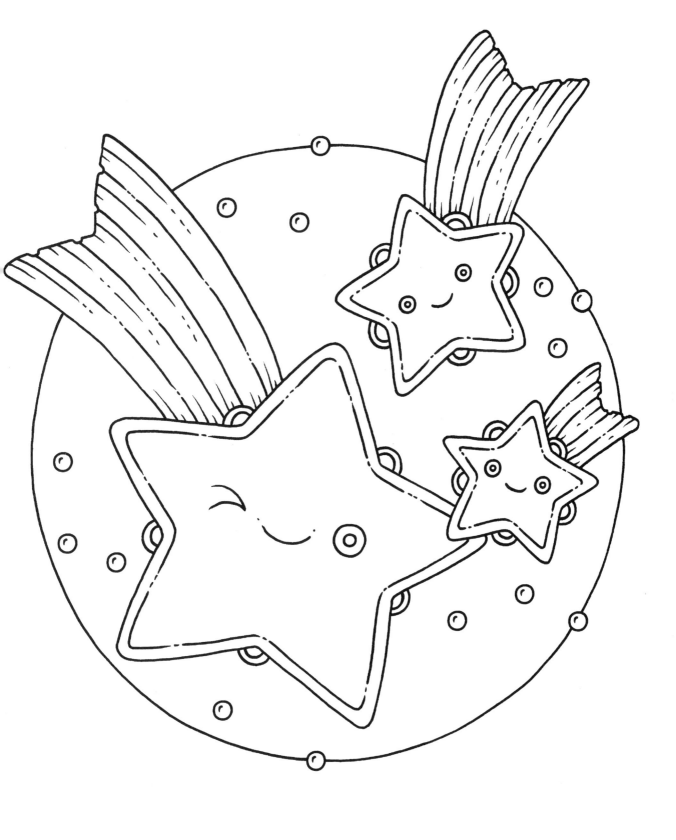

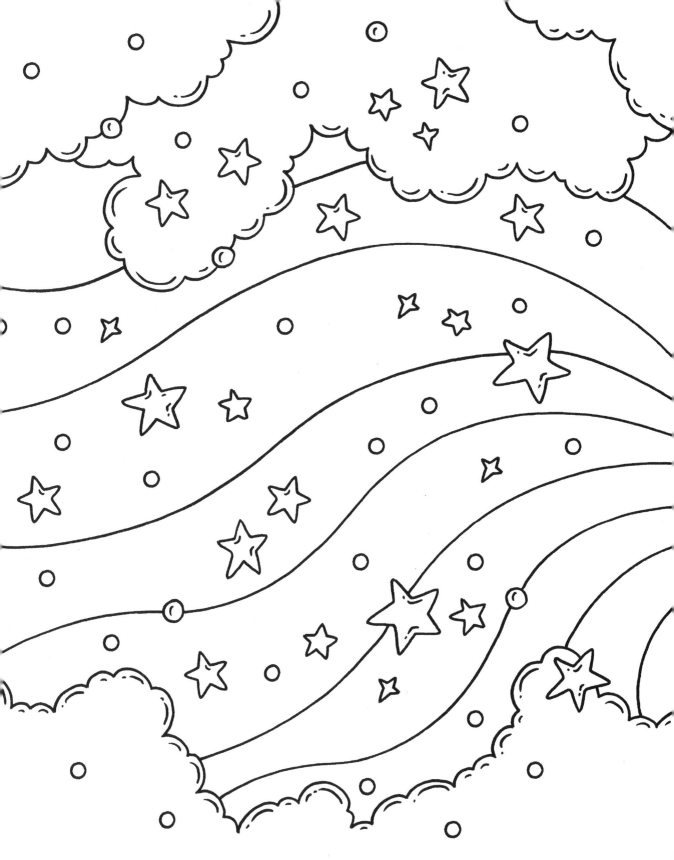

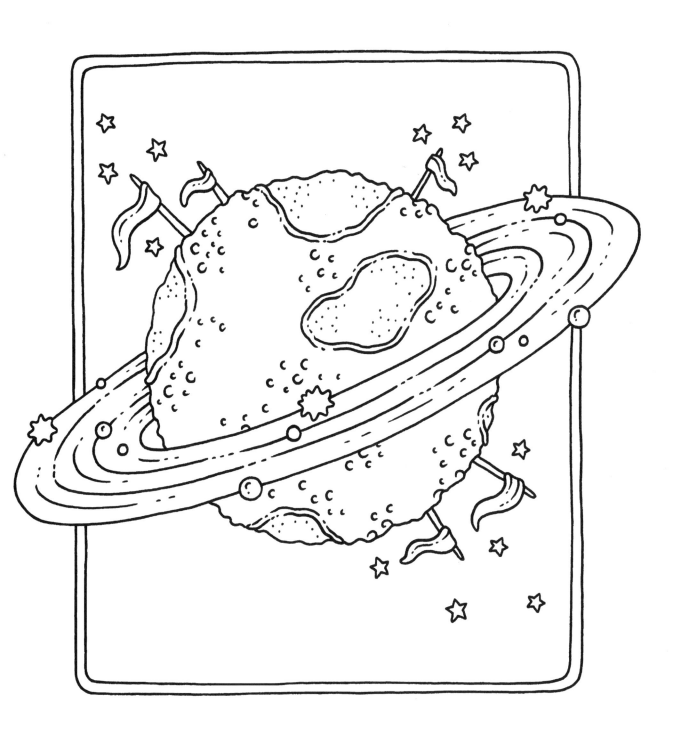

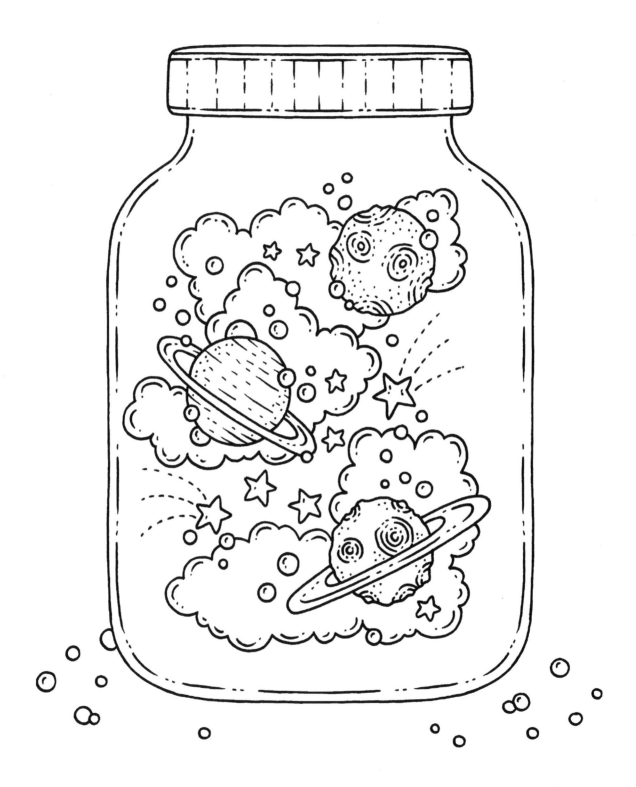